LIFE

Holy Lands

One Place Three Faiths

Judaism

It is the oldest of the three great monotheistic religions. Judaism's view of history, as rendered in the Torah some 2,600 years ago, provided a basis for Christianity and, later, Islam. The Israeli leader Moses, who received the Lord's laws atop Mount Sinai—perhaps this very summit on the Sinai Peninsula—is a revered prophet in all three faiths.

LIFE
Holy Lands

Christianity

In Israel, 2,000 years ago, a child was born to a Jewish couple. Jesus grew to be a charismatic preacher, gathering disciples as he went. This Son of God performed miracles, they said: raising the dead, calming these waters of Galilee. Jerusalem's authorities, perceiving a threat, had Jesus executed. His followers, taking up the cross, built the world's largest religion in his name.

LIFE

Holy Lands

One Place Three Faiths

Islam

More than 1,300 years ago, a man in Mecca was visited by the archangel Gabriel and received an extraordinary gift: the word from Allah, the one God. Muhammad, according to Muslims, was the prophet presaged by Moses, and Muhammad's book, the Koran, represented the ultimate truth. Taking his message across the desert to Medina, near these hills, he created Islam.

Kazuyoshi Nomachi/PPS

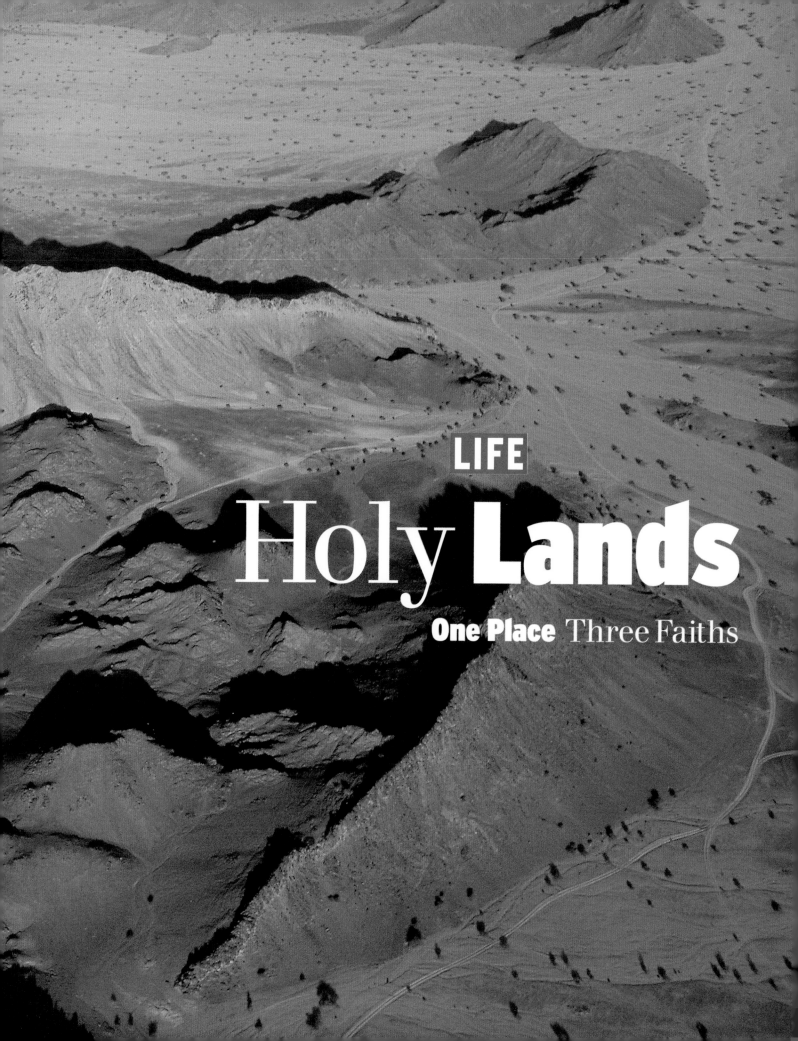

LIFE

Holy Lands

One Place Three Faiths

LIFE

Editor Robert Sullivan
Creative Director Ian Denning
Picture Editor Barbara Baker Burrows
Executive Editor Robert Andreas
Associate Picture Editors
Christina Lieberman, Vivette Porges
Senior Reporter Hildegard Anderson
Writer/Reporter Lauren Nathan
Copy J.C. Choi (Chief), Stacy Sabraw
Production Manager Michael Roseman
Picture Research Lauren Steel
Photo Assistant Joshua Colow
Consulting Picture Editor (London)
Suzanne Hodgart

Publisher Andrew Blau
Director of Business Development Marta Bialek
Finance Director Camille Sanabria
Assistant Finance Manager Karen Tortora

Time Inc. Home Entertainment

President Rob Gursha
Vice President, Branded Businesses
David Arfine
Executive Director, Marketing Services
Carol Pittard
Director, Retail & Special Sales
Tom Mifsud
Director of Finance Tricia Griffin
Marketing Director Kenneth Maehlum
Assistant Director Ann Marie Doherty
Prepress Manager Emily Rabin
Book Production Manager
Jonathan Polsky
Associate Product Manager
Jennifer Dowell

Special thanks to Suzanne DeBenedetto,
Robert Dente, Gina Di Meglio,
Anne-Michelle Gallero, Peter Harper,
Natalie McCrea, Jessica McGrath,
Mary Jane Rigoroso, Steven Sandonato,
Bozena Szwagulinski, Niki Whelan

Published by

LIFE Books

Time Inc. 1271 Avenue of the Americas, New York, NY 10020

Library of Congress Control Number: 2002106438
ISBN: 1-929049-86-2

"LIFE" is a trademark of Time Inc.

We welcome your comments and suggestions
about LIFE Books. Please write to us at:
LIFE Books, Attention: Book Editors,
PO Box 11016, Des Moines, IA 50336-1016

If you would like to order any of our hardcover Collector's Edition
books, please call us at 1-800-327-6388. (Monday through Friday,
7:00 a.m.–8:00 p.m. or Saturday, 7:00 a.m.–6:00 p.m. Central Time).

Please visit us, and sample past editions of LIFE, at www.LIFE.com.

Jerusalem

**In Hebrew it is Yerushalayim, in Arabic Bayt al-Muqaddas. It is 3,800 years
old, and if it has been controlled politically by Israel since 1967, it remains
a spiritual stronghold of three great religions: Judaism, Christianity and
Islam. A place of prophets, martyrs, tension and turmoil, Jerusalem holds
the promise of life eternal—and the lurking prospect of sudden death.**

Denis Waugh

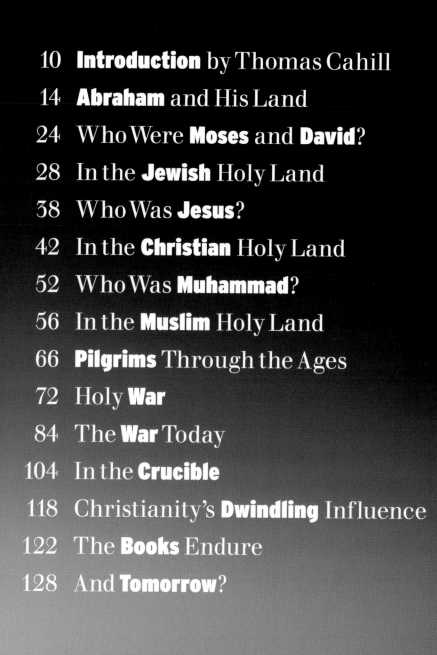

One Land Three Paths

By Thomas Cahill

And a great sign appeared in the heavens,
bearing the symbols of the three Abrahamic
*   religions:*
a shining star that streamed six points,
an upright pole of timber crossed by a horizontal
*   beam,*
and a glowing crescent moon.
And the three symbols were linked together
by nearly invisible bands of gold
to form one sign.
And a voice rang out:
These are my children, linked together by bands
*   they cannot see,*
all children of the one Father.
And though they call me by different names,
I have one name common to all.

For Peace is the Name of God.

Whether the idea comes to us in a vision, as above, or as the final step in a series of rational thoughts on the subject of Judaism, Christianity, and Islam in the world of the 21st century, whether in prayer or meditation, in discourse or dialogue, no one who considers the subject for long can fail to come to the conclusion that sincere men and women—Jews, Christians and Muslims—must find fresh ways to bridge ancient divisions and modern hatreds and to link our three religions together more closely, while each remains itself, losing nothing of its essence but gaining strength from its links to the others.

Whatever may happen in the short term, whatever fresh horrors may transpire, no one can doubt that in the long run there will be peace in the Holy Land, a peace of which all reasonable men and women can already sketch the bold outlines: a definitive end to violence on both sides, agreed borders with open democracy and transparent government on both sides, dismantling of colonial settlements, withdrawal of occupying forces, just compensation of refugees, mutual security arrangements, some form of shared sovereignty over Jerusalem, a regional economic consortium on the model of the first steps taken to create the European Union, and lastly, perhaps even a unified, if federated, foreign policy. Since there is no way to separate Israelis and Palestinians for all time by a new Berlin Wall, they must together find the ways to reconcile the irreconcilable.

The only alternative to this is mutual destruction, the outlines of which we can also sketch: increasing violence, both terrorist and state-sponsored, the end of Israel's democracy as it becomes a racist fortress state, a conflagration of the whole region, one that will leave the Middle East (and no doubt places far beyond the Middle East) looking like the charred emptiness that immense asteroids left on Earth in prehistoric times.

If you are Palestinian, you are likely to feel that none of the above give sufficient space to Palestinian grievances; if you are Israeli, you are likely to feel that none of the above take with sufficient seriousness Israel's just claims and the unspeakable horrors the Jews have endured through 2,000 years of Western history and now in their tiny, besieged state. You would be right, whether Palestinian or Israeli. There is no way that I in this brief introduction can do justice to either side. But you would be wrong, as well, if you promote only your own arguments. The problem of all unresolvable conflicts is the same, whether in Northern Ireland, central Africa, the Balkans or the Middle East: Each side makes the same one-sided claim, "Only *my* wounds matter."

The solution is dialogue, dialogue that truly takes the Other into account. Yossi Klein Halevi has called interfaith dialogue "the true spiritual adven-

Thomas Cahill is the author of *How the Irish Saved Civilization, The Gifts of the Jews, Desire of the Everlasting Hills: The World Before and After Jesus,* and, most recently, *Pope John XXIII.*

ture of our generation. For the first time, believers can experience something of the inner life of other religions while remaining faithful to their own." But such dialogue must always be preceded (and accompanied) by two exceedingly difficult processes: adequate self-criticism and genuine appreciation of the Other.

Self-criticism is a serious business and seldom a successful exercise. I am reminded of the "high-toned Christian woman" who came to an ecumenical gathering ready, in what she thought of as her expansive generosity, to forgive all that other denominations had done to hers. But she was shocked and outraged on finding that she was expected to be ready, not only to forgive, but to be forgiven!

As a Catholic Christian, I know that my own denomination was militantly unwilling to criticize itself before the pontificate of John XXIII, by far the

greatest of all popes, who reigned for less than five years and died in 1963, his fabulous revolution incomplete. Though subsequent popes, particularly the present one, John Paul II, have made real strides in naming and apologizing for the horrendous sins of Christians toward both Jews and Muslims, even *his* historical analysis lets Christians—and, especially, Catholics and, more especially, popes—squirm off the hook too easily. We still have a long way to go to create the golden bands that should unite Christianity to these other monotheistic religions. And in regard to other besetting sins of Catholicism—clericalism, institutional fascism, episcopal hypocrisy, sexual oppression (the list is far too long to enumerate fully)—no pope, except the incredible John XXIII, has even named them.

Yet each side in the dialogue must take rigorous stock of itself and be willing to see its limitations and failures for what they have been and what

Some are trying: On the outer wall of Jerusalem's Old City in 2001, a sign with symbols of the three religions urges peace—and also announces a nearby outdoor art exhibit on the theme of coexistence.

they continue to be. The real enemy of self-criticism is self-confirming sanctimony, a trait all religious traditions are well supplied with. Jesus spoke words of universal application when he said: "Judge not, that ye be not judged. For with what judgment ye judge, ye shall be judged: and with what measure ye mete, it shall be measured to you again. And why beholdest thou the mote that is in thy brother's eye, but considerest not the beam that is in thine own eye?" With this is mind, I leave unremarked whatever flaws I find in other traditions. I stick to my own, quite flawed tradition—and leave it to you, dear Reader, to consider the beam in your own eye.

The second ingredient necessary for successful dialogue is genuine appreciation of the Other. It is possible. I have just returned from a wonderful conference in Palermo, Italy, sponsored (as it is each year in different cities) by the Community of Sant'Egidio, a worldwide ecumenical society of ordinary laypeople who befriend the poor and attempt to alleviate political and religious tensions wherever they can. (These inspired amateurs are famous for negotiating a peace in Mozambique after 16 years of bloody combat between guerrillas and the government that left a million dead, a peace that has now lasted almost as long as the war.) This year's conference was devoted especially to a dialogue among the three monotheisms Judaism, Christianity and Islam. Throughout the days of the conference, one could see distinguished representatives of these three (and many other) religions breaking bread together, exhibiting quiet warmth and affection for one another, all encouraged by the immense generosity of our hosts and the spectacular setting in which we found ourselves, hemmed in by the Mediterranean and the great, all-encompassing rock of Monte Pellegrino, and moving through this history-haunted place that exhibits on every corner, in everything from classical metopes to ancient icons, from jagged Hebrew inscriptions to intricate arabesques, its living ties to every Mediterranean culture. The conference ended with a music-backed affirmation from all the participants that they would work tirelessly on behalf of peace, which "is the Name of God."

A gathering of clerics from various faiths presents an image of ecumenical brotherhood at the Palermo conference. The meeting was dedicated to bridging the gaps between the monotheisms, and Cahill returned from Italy believing, "It is possible."

The closing ceremony, as Daniel Kropf, a genial Israeli businessman, said, was "one of the most moving things you will ever see on this earth." The candle-lighting ritual that concludes the final ceremony—candles lighted by all the religious representatives, many in their most extravagantly colorful robes—was brought to its end this year by three prominent clergymen, a dignified imam (Moroccan theologian Mohammed Amine Smaili), a diminutive Vatican official in charge of dialogue with Jews and with other Christians (Walter Kasper, known as "Kasper the Friendly Cardinal"), and a rabbi who looked the embodiment of the wisdom of the ages (René Samuel Sirat, chief rabbi emeritus of Europe), all lighting the same candle together. This was the image that all participants could not help but take away with them.

To spark the possibility of some new approaches to the Other, I would like to leave you not with my words but with the sounds of voices from different traditions, all heard—if not in person, at least in quotation—in Palermo. What harmony these voices can achieve singing together.

“ Among the positive peripheral outcrops of the September 11 events, there is the heightened desire of many in the West to learn about Islam and better understand its principles and perspective on life and the universe . . . An important occasion has thus presented itself which the Islamic world needs to seize upon, with a view to project their faith and civilization and their objectives and conception of relations with others . . . In order to do so, we have to inaugurate between ourselves a positive dialogue not only to overcome the current crisis, which we see as transitory, but also to establish the foundations of dialogue for our future and for the sake of posterity. That is why we would want this dialogue to be also a strategic one that takes into account the basic economic as well as the political interests. ”

— **Abdelouahed Belkeziz**,
Secretary General of the Organization of the Islamic Conference to the Joint OIC-EU Forum on Civilization and Harmony

“ Laying the foundations for one world is the most important task of our time. These foundations are not negotiated statements and agreements. These foundations are, rather, in the stockpiling of trust through dialogue and the creation of relationships that can sustain both agreements and disagreements. Moving forward . . . in dialogue with those other faiths we will create the foundational relationship of One World. Moving forward alone, we will not. ”

— **Diana Eck**, Harvard Divinity School

“ All human beings are like the organs of a body:
when one is afflicted with pain,
the others cannot rest in peace. ”

— **Sadi Shirazi**, Medieval Iranian poet

“ Nothing has proved harder in civilization than seeing God or good or dignity in those unlike ourselves. There are surely many ways of arriving at that generosity of spirit, and each faith may need to find its own way. I propose that the truth at the heart of monotheism is that God is greater than religion, that God is only partially comprehended by any one faith . . . What would such a [broader] faith be like? It would be like being secure in my own home and yet moved by the beauty of a foreign place knowing that while it is not my home, it is still part of the glory of the world that is ours. It would be knowing that we are sentences in the story of our people but that there are other stories, each written by God out of the letters of lives bound together in community. Those who are confident of their faith are not threatened but enlarged by the different faiths of others. In the midst of our multiple insecurities, we need now the confidence to recognize the irreducible, glorious dignity of difference. ”

— **Jonathan Sacks**, Chief Rabbi
of the British Commonwealth

Amen.

It was at the Dead Sea that Sodom and Gomorrah fell. Lot, the nephew of Abraham, escaped, but his disobedient wife was turned into a pillar of salt. Some say this outcropping is Lot's wife.

Abraham and His Land

He, as much as any this side of the supreme deity, belongs to them all. The shared beliefs of Judaism, Christianity and Islam include a single god, Adam and Eve, and a common roster of holy people—most importantly, Abraham.

The reasons for contemplating the holy lands of Judaism, Christianity and Islam at this time are evident. In a region forever plagued by territorial disputes, the recent heightened violence between Arabs and Jews—punctuated in 2002 by a horrific series of suicide bombings and Israeli crackdowns in the West Bank—begs for an understanding of the roots of conflict. The fruitlessness of Pope John Paul II's pilgrimages to Jordan and Israel in the spring of 2000, during which he apologized for past Roman Catholic misdeeds against other religions and pleaded for ecumenical compassion among all faiths, brings into question what influence Christianity retains in the land of Christ's birth.

And for Americans, there is, of course, September 11. Radical Islamists said forcefully that the events of that day were about religion, about Western infidels transgressing on sacred soil in Saudi Arabia, about Muhammad's true teachings, about the need for global jihad. What did the message of September 11 really have to do with Islam, and how does that apply to what's going on week by week,

day by day, hour by hour, in Jerusalem, Bethlehem, Hebron, Ramallah and, indeed, Riyadh, Rome, Washington, D.C.?

The complexity of the equation is daunting, and certainly some answers cannot be known. For example, What is the difference between the devout believer, the fundamentalist and the radical? Through whose eyes are we looking when we make that determination?

There are things we cannot fathom and things that will have a different cast tomorrow than today. Nevertheless it is worthwhile to seek a basic understanding of the faiths involved: where they came from, their shared place, their shared history, some of their shared traditions, their different hopes and dreams for the future of their holy land. In assessing the Middle East today, it's not unreasonable to conclude that Judaism, Christianity and Islam are as different as the moon, the stars and the planets, and as antagonistic as dogs and cats. In deep history, however, nothing is further from the truth. In deep history, they are one.

This argument could start with Yahweh or God or Allah, the single sacred being who is the heart

Three views of Abraham's test: In an 18th century Jewish painting (below) and a Rembrandt from the 17th century, Abraham prepares to slay Isaac. In a Turkish illustration, circa 1583, he raises his knife to Ishmael. The Koran does not specify which son God asked Abraham to sacrifice, but Muslims consider Ishmael to be the designee and Mecca, rather than Jerusalem, the site.

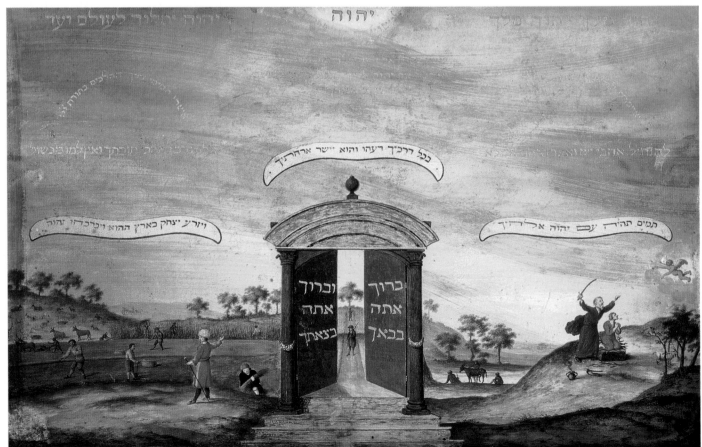

alone in teaching that their original sin had to be redeemed by Christ's crucifixion).

But while freely admitting that there is no way to address this topic in a rigorously secular manner, it is most useful to begin with an historical human being (who may or may not have existed; proving him is impossible) named Abraham.

Or Abram, as he appears in the earliest citations. These are in Genesis, in both the Hebrew and Christian Bibles, documents whose early chapters are also shared tradition with Islam. (The Koran, Islam's holy text as composed by Muhammad in the 7th century A.D., cites and sanctions many biblical characters and stories; until the time of Abraham, it is in general accord with biblical accounts of how things went.) According to Genesis, "Abram," a name referring to "father love" or an exaltation of the father, was one of Noah's 10th-generation descendants and was born in the Mesopotamian city of Ur (today, in the most prominent theory, Ur is Iraq's Tall al-Muqayyar, 200 miles southeast of

and soul of all three religions. Before the rise of Judaism, Christianity and Islam, it was deviant thought that there was not a plurality of gods but, rather, one supreme being. Today, by contrast, more than half the planet adheres to a one-god theology, with 2 billion Christians, 1.3 billion Muslims and nearly 15 million Jews outnumbering the followers of pantheistic religions.

So this argument could start with God, or it could begin with Adam and Eve, humanity's progenitors in all three faiths (even if Christianity is

Excavations near Ur have revealed a city dating from circa 2000 B.C.—approximately the time of Abraham. From what was then a port on the Persian Gulf (Ur is now inland), Abraham went forth.

Mediterranean
Sea

Zoan

Cairo

Memphis

E G Y P T

Nile

Thebes

Baghdad). In 2000, John Paul tried desperately to add Ur to his itinerary and said at one point that no Christian's Holy Land pilgrimage could be complete without a visit to Abraham's birthplace, but the Pope was rebuffed by Saddam Hussein.

According to the Bible's genealogies, and other historical writings measured against modern archaeological finds, it seems probable that Abraham, if he existed at all, lived sometime between 2100 and 1500 B.C. This was not a godless age in places such as Ur; it was a multi-god age. How Abram's thinking evolved to monotheism—and thereby put him in position to become the first patriarch of both the people of Israel and the Arabs—is speculative. Most of Ur looked up to a moon god named Sin, but Abram would be different.

According to scripture, his clan was migratory even before God gave Abram instructions to travel yet farther, and because of who he would become in the theologies of great religions, every step he and his people took served to sanctify holy ground. First they went west from Ur to Haran, between the Tigris and Euphrates rivers in northern Mesopotamia. Haran, which today is in Turkey, was a site of pil-

grimage for Sin worshipers, and so an expected destination for citizens from Ur. Abram's father, Terah, died in Haran at the age of 205, says the Bible. The good genes of his family would prove essential in the Abraham story, as will shortly be evident.

Abram's caravan, which included not only his wife Sarai but his biblically famous nephew Lot, went west again and forded the Euphrates, perhaps at Carchemish. Nayrab, near Aleppo, was another Sin city, and probably a stopping point. As new fields offered new opportunities of fortune to the itinerant shepherds, the journey continued: Damascus (probably), Shechem, Bethel (now Baytin, north of Jerusalem), southwest to Egypt and then back to the oaks of Mamre, which, according to Genesis, "are at Hebron." According to modern knowledge, they were a mile and a half northwest of Hebron, at a place now called Ramat al-Khalil, Arabic for "Heights of the Friend," Allah's friend being Abram. Amidst the oaks of Mamre, events of significance transpired, leading to narratives that would change the world.

Lot and his family were attacked, and Abram leapt into action, speeding northeast from Mamre

David Lees

Satellite Photograph: Photo Researchers

TURKEY

Carchemish — Haran

Aleppo

CYPRUS

Hamath

SYRIA

Euphrates

Tigris

Mari

IRAN

Beirut

LEBANON

Damascus

Baghdad

ISRAEL

IRAQ

Babylon

Bethel

Amman

Jerusalem

Dead Sea

Hebron

Erech

Ancient Coastline

Sodom and Gomorrah

Ur

JORDAN

Basra

SAUDI

KUWAIT

ARABIA

Kuwait

Persian Gulf

Medina

Red Sea

Mecca

The Path of Abraham

At the behest of God, Abraham traveled from his native Mesopotamia into Canaan, between Syria and Egypt. In following his footsteps today, it is evident that the patriarch's progress passes through countries that have evolved in quite different ways. The route above shows Abraham's path as it is delineated in the Hebrew Bible. The Muslim account, which offers some additional details regarding his wanderings, does have Abraham settling near where he built the Kaaba, in Mecca.

Abraham's Path ←	**Ancient City** ● Babylon	
Modern Border —	**Modern City** Baghdad	

He was a city kid who became part of a nomadic caravan. In crossing what is now Judea, Abraham and his fellow shepherds would seek out fields with some fertility in the vast, fallow desert.

to save him, showing a warrior instinct in one who theretofore was largely pacifist. This enlarges his character but does not fundamentally change his role, his being. What did transform him—and, thus, everything—was the call from God to forsake his old country and to found a new nation in Canaan, between Mesopotamia and Egypt. If Abram took up this considerable task, he would be blessed with many offspring, and his "seed" would inherit what he surveyed. God pledged to Abram that if his people remained faithful, then Canaan, which included the modern Palestine, would be their "everlasting possession [Gen. 17:4–9]."

To this rough point in time, the Bible and the Koran do not vigorously disagree. Genesis and Muhammad's account of Allah's words in the Koran are in basic accord about who Abram was and what was promised to him. It is with the man's sons that the stories diverge.

Abram was 75 years old when he entered into his covenant with God, who in a later vision certified the agreement by changing Abram's name to Abraham, meaning "Father of many nations." In the immediate aftermath of the first revelation, Abraham and Sarah, as she was renamed, remained childless, and what might come of the communication with God was uncertain. Sarah lent her Egyptian handmaiden, Hagar, to Abraham that she might bear him a child. This boy was Ishmael.

God continued to talk with Abraham; their debate about Sodom and Gomorrah, with Abraham urging leniency for the sinful cities, was a notable dialogue. (God, while moved by Abraham's arguments, destroyed the wicked citadels, though he spared Lot, who at the time was living in Sodom.) When Abraham was 99, God pledged him a son with Sarah. A year later she bore Isaac.

When she became a mother, Sarah insisted that her husband banish Hagar and Ishmael from his community, and Abraham obeyed. To greatly simplify the latter chapters of Abraham's story: In Genesis, God tests Abraham's faith by asking him to sacrifice Isaac. Abraham is on the verge of doing so atop Mount Moriah when God stays his hand, pro-

Above and below: Jews honor their heritage at the Tomb of the Patriarchs in Hebron, where Abraham, Sarah, and Isaac and his son Jacob are said to rest. Opposite: Abraham's failure to sway God is memorialized in this desolate land on the Dead Sea where it is said that Sodom and Gomorrah lie buried.

vides a ram as a substitute sacrifice and allows Isaac to grow, prosper and, through his son Jacob (who will be called Israel), to found the Jewish nation in Palestine. According to Islam, it was Ishmael who was nearly sacrificed. His many offspring settled on the site of the future Mecca, where they flourished, spreading across the Arab world: the Muslims.

Abraham died at the age of 175 and was buried beside his wife in the Cave of Machpelah east of Mamre, which is today in the West Bank.

So Abraham was indeed the patriarch of many nations built beneath two overarching theologies: Judaism and Islam. As for his place in the Christian world, John Paul's high regard for the prophet is indicative. Abraham is cited 72 times in the New Testament, more than any Old Testament figure save Moses, and always with the utmost respect. No less an authority than St. Paul, in ardent admiration of Abraham's righteousness and pristine faith, speaks of him as "the father of us all [Rom. 4:16]."

The great religious saga in the Middle East starts with him, with Abraham. Where it will lead, we still do not know.

To Jews he is Moshe Rabbenu (Moses, Our Teacher), lawgiver, hero above all heroes; to Christians he is a model of faith; to Muslims, Musa is the first prophet to herald the coming of Muhammad. For Christians and Muslims, subsequent leaders Jesus and Muhammad delivered modified teachings that took precedence, but for Jews, whose Messiah is yet to come, Moses remains preeminent. "The most solitary and most powerful hero in biblical history," Elie Wiesel called Moses. "After him, nothing else was the same again."

He is said to have lived 3,200 years ago, in the time of Egyptian pharaoh Ramses II. Proving his existence has, as with Abraham, been impossible. Some scholars point out that several chapters in the Moses saga, beginning with the story of a baby in an ark woven of reeds, are similar to older Mesopotamian and Egyptian legends. So what? Even if Moses or aspects of him were borrowed, there are in the story entirely original philosophies. And, at its end, a revolutionary moral. Moses certainly seems real, and the detail and complexity of his personality—right down to a speech impediment—may be the strongest argument that such a man did exist. Moses is exceedingly human: weak and strong, brave yet tormented by doubt, a rebel but a faithful follower, a warrior and a saint.

He begins his life as a Hebrew born in Egypt during a time of persecution. Hebrew adults there were forced into slavery: "harsh labor at mortar and bricks." When the burgeoning Israelites became even more of a problem in Pharaoh's eyes, even an infant's lot became dire: It was decreed

Who Were
Moses and David?

One was a great prophet and teacher who delivered Yahweh's laws to his people. The other was a renowned warrior and king. One was the savior of Israel, while the other unified the Israeli nation and gave it direction.

that newborn males were to be thrown into the Nile. Moses' mother tried hiding her boy, but after several weeks she grew desperate, and left him by the water's edge. The baby was rescued by Pharaoh's daughter and raised as her son.

Life in Egypt was not bad for Moses, but it was intolerable for his blood kinsmen. One day, Moses saw an Egyptian beating a Hebrew. Moses, believing there were no witnesses about, struck and killed the Egyptian. He fled to the land of Midian, where he met Zipporah, daughter of Jethro. He and Zipporah married and had two sons, but this was not

to be the whole of Moses' family. His clan would encompass all members of all tribes within the Israeli nation.

A bush was aflame, and yet—impossibly—it was not consumed. "Moses! Moses!" A voice was calling from the burning bush. "I have marked well the plight of My people in Egypt and have heeded their outcry . . . I have come down to rescue them from the Egyptians." The voice belonged to Yahweh or, rather, YHWH, a Hebrew word that may have derived from "to be"; it became so holy that it could not be pronounced but only read aloud as

In the reception hall of the Knesset, Israel's Parliament in Jerusalem, hang three tapestries created in the 1960s by Jewish artist Marc Chagall. The central tapestry depicts the gathering of Hebrew exiles, with David (left) and Moses in principal roles.

Working in different media, Chagall rendered David and Bathsheba in oil (1962-63, above) and Moses and the Burning Bush in glass (1962-68, opposite). Born to a poor family in Russia in 1887, the artist was raised in the Hasidic culture and, even after gaining fame in Paris, never forgot his roots: The Chagall museum in Nice is dedicated to "the Biblical Message."

Adonai, "Lord." Yahweh's plan involved Moses, but Moses was not necessarily willing. "Who am I?" to take on this task. Conquering his fears, he approached Pharaoh and demanded that his people be let go, but he was rebuffed. Moses then told his brother, Aaron, to touch the Nile with his staff, and the river turned to blood. Then the plagues descended and Egypt was overrun by frogs, flies, hail, locusts, "a darkness that can be touched" and other miseries. Yahweh's 10th infliction was to kill all firstborn Egyptian males.

Next: Exodus. On the run, Moses parted the Red Sea (in proper translation, the Sea of Reeds—perhaps Sabkhet el Bardowil, a lagoon on the northeastern shore of the Sinai, not far from the Mediterranean Sea). The Israelites passed safely across the dry land, then turned and watched as Pharaoh's soldiers were engulfed by the inrushing water. Moses' people were free.

In their continued quest for the Promised Land, Yahweh provided for them. Manna fell from heaven when food ran out in the wilderness; Moses drew water from a rock to quench their thirst. In return, Yahweh asked obedience, and atop Mount Sinai gave Moses the rules, the commandments—the "ten pearls," as ancient rabbis called them. Although Moses himself would not reach the Promised Land, he pointed the way for his people.

Some two centuries after Moses, the prophet Samuel, with an eye toward uniting the disorganized tribal federation that was the Israeli nation, anointed Saul as king. Saul alternately succeeded and stumbled, was exuberant or depressed, depending on whether he was in or out of the Lord's grace. Tired of Saul's flawed religiosity, God directed Samuel to Bethlehem to seek out a man named Jesse: "I have decided on one of his sons to be king." The chosen one was Jesse's youngest, David, a shepherd boy. Samuel "took the horn of oil and anointed him in the presence of his brothers; and the spirit of the Lord gripped David from that day on [1 Sam. 16:13]."

David entered Saul's service soon after, first as a lyre player retained to assuage the king's despondency, then as a warrior. No one could be found to fight the Philistine Goliath of Gath, a 10-foot-tall mountain of menace—until David. He entered the field of battle with only a sling and stones. Goliath sneered, but David said boldly, "You come against me with sword and spear and javelin; but I come against you in the name of the Lord of Hosts." David's first shot found its mark, the giant fell, and as David took Goliath's sword to behead the man, the Philistine army fled.

David's fame among the Israelites was instant and immense. The tragic Saul now worried that he had a challenger in his midst. The king made attempts on David's life, and David finally fled the court. More than once, he sought refuge among the Philistines, then he and his army were on the move when he received word that Saul had died after a battle at Mount Gilboa. The remnants of Saul's army could not compete with David's increasingly powerful forces, and in about 1000 B.C. the tribal elders, meeting at Hebron, established David as king of Israel. David relocated to Jerusalem, which he named as his capital. In subsequent battles he drove the Philistines back into Philistia, conquered several Canaanite cities and expanded Israel's reach and power. David made Israel great.

Not wanting to fall out of favor with Yahweh, as had Saul, David carefully combined state with church. He saw the symbolism of relocating the sacred Ark of the Covenant, which contained the Ten Commandments, from Kiriathjearim to Jerusalem. He collected dozens of psalms for worship. He stayed loyal to God, and the prophet Nathan said to David, "Your house and your kingship shall ever be secure before you; your throne shall be established forever [2 Sam. 7:16]."

David, like Moses, was only too human— women being his weakness. He married one of Saul's daughters, had a son with each of six wives in Hebron, then took other wives and concubines in Jerusalem. Bathsheba was the wife of one of David's soldiers when she became pregnant by the king, whom she married after her husband's death in battle. God was not pleased with David's behavior, and the infant died. Bathsheba and David had a second son, Solomon, and he was nominated by his father as the royal successor. This was sanctioned by Yahweh. Circa 961 B.C., "David slept with his fathers, and he was buried in the City of David"—having unified a nation.

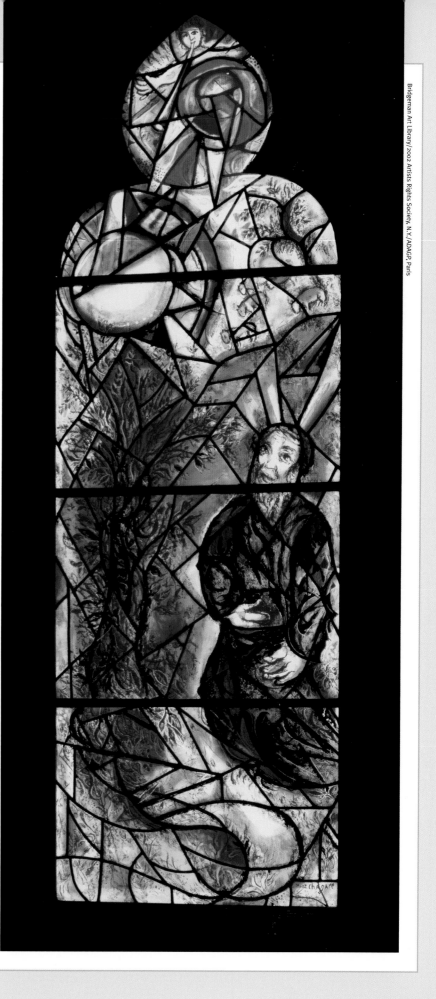

Is this what Moses surveyed just before he received the word of the Lord? As with much biblical history, this is conjecture; belief is a matter of faith. There is more than one Mount Sinai in the Middle East, including a famous peak on the Sinai Peninsula from which this photograph was taken. There are at least eight places that could have been the setting for the story of Moses and the Ten Commandments.

In the **Jewish** Holy Land

Throughout the Middle East, temples, tombs and ancient
fortresses mark the passage of prophets and kings.

The first king of Israel reigned for about two decades some 3,000 years ago. Saul was the son of Kish, a prosperous member of the tribe of Benjamin, and was made king by the 12 tribes of Israel. Saul's brilliance lay on the battlefield, where he inspired a largely volunteer army to repeated success against the Philistines. Yet he could not deliver the coup de grâce, and it was on Mount Gilboa, seen here beyond the Valley of Jezreel, that Saul and three of his sons died in combat with the Philistines. In his elegy, Saul's successor, David, said: "The beauty of Israel is slain upon thy high places: how are the mighty fallen!"

Richard T. Nowitz

Jerusalem's Temple Mount was the site of the First Temple, built by Solomon, as well as the Second Temple, raised by Herod the Great. All that remains from the latter is part of a retaining wall from its courtyard, known as the Western Wall. (Gentiles sometimes call it the Wailing Wall, owing to the lamentations there, but many Jews consider the name undignified.) Note its proximity to the Dome of the Rock.

The traditional King David's tomb (above) is in a nondescript building on Mount Zion in Jerusalem. (There are those, however, who believe that the Zion site may actually be an early Judeo-Christian synagogue.) Left: The Ark of the Covenant, a wooden chest that contained the Ten Commandments, was kept here in Shiloh before it was captured by the Philistines. At right, these steps leading to the Temple Mount were ascended by King David.

Richard T. Nowitz (2)

Denis Waugh

Richard T. Nowitz (2)

At the Dead Sea stands Masada (above). In the first century B.C., Herod the Great built a fortress atop the mesa, and later, a thousand men, women and children held out for two years against a Roman army 15 times larger. Masada remains a symbol of pride for Jews. In 1947 a Bedouin shepherd made a stunning find in the cliffs of Qumran (opposite): the Dead Sea Scrolls, manuscripts that shed light on rabbinic Judaism and links between Jewish and early Christian traditions.

Who Was **Jesus**?

A Jewish carpenter's son born to humble circumstances, he grew to become a charismatic preacher who espoused radical philosophies. His words attracted a handful of followers and then, in the centuries following, billions.

Hans Memling, born near Frankfurt am Main circa 1430, was a portraitist and painter of Christian imagery; during his career in Brussels and Bruges, he revisited certain crucial episodes in Jesus' life. Of his depictions of Mary with Jesus, the one above, painted between 1470 and 1472, is the most intimate, with no instrument-playing angels in attendance.

He was descended from Abraham through the line of Isaac, as it extended through David. So says the New Testament of the Christian Bible, which concerns itself with the life of Jesus: born to Mary and Joseph, the Christ, God's son made flesh. His people were from Nazareth, but two Gospel authors are agreed that he was born in Bethlehem. Angels and a shining star signaled that his was a special nativity; still, nothing in Jesus' life presaged the phenomenon that would follow his brief time on earth, which may have been as short as 33 years.

The earthly son of a carpenter, Jesus seemed ready to follow in the family trade but then showed a precocity for philosophy and teaching, lecturing even his elders and senior clerics. If his message offended some, it was alluring to others; he was, in an era crowded with prophets, soothsayers, doomsayers and Zealots, especially charismatic. Jesus' thinking was radical. At a time when there was not only strong-arm rule by kings but also, in the streets, greed, violence and lawlessness, notions of pacifism and charity were alien. The idea of giving one's cloak to a needy stranger—a *brother,* Jesus suggested—did not have much currency in Palestine before he existed. Even religions that would reject him as the Son of God, including Judaism and Islam, would later admire many of his sociological theories. These rules for living were and remain exquisite, and in fact, many of Allah's teachings as rendered by Muhammad some 600 years later are not unlike those of Jesus in their compassion, selflessness and social unorthodoxy.

As Jesus gained followers and notoriety, things began to be said about him: that he performed miracles, walked on water, fed a multitude with mea-

Eric Lessing/Art Resource

Szépművészeti Muzeum, Budapest

ger rations, raised the dead. In the New Testament, these stories are not presented for their supernatural effect but rather to forward a moral point or to instill faith. They certainly rallied Jesus' disciples, who started whispering, "He's the one." This was dangerous for all concerned.

Jesus, courting fate, went to Jerusalem at a time when his ministry was no longer a secret to the city's hierarchy. With him traveled a small group of loyal apostles—including one who would betray him—and a slightly larger group of camp followers. Tormented, Jesus secluded himself to contemplate what was about to be set in motion. He returned to his friends, telling them during supper that there was a traitor in their midst. This was Judas, who subsequently identified Jesus for local authorities. Jesus was condemned for blasphemy, tortured and then crucified on the hill at Calvary, outside Jerusalem. He was buried in a rock tomb

Memling, who in his lifetime was called "the most skillful painter in the whole of Christendom," gained just and lasting fame. He was often copied, and a debate still rages over how much current Memling is Memling. Most critics feel that at least 20 major works are authentic, and that the artist's reputation is secure based upon that oeuvre. These pages show a copy of a Memling triptych depicting Christ's persecution, crucifixion and resurrection.

by Joseph of Arimathea. The New Testament tells of Jesus' resurrection three days later and a direct ascension to heaven, where he and the father, God, await the ultimate judgment day of all mankind.

In the immediate aftermath of Jesus' death, there was no predicting that his cult would survive any longer than the others that were then receiving attention. But his philosophy was so profound, his message so attractive, and his succeeding generations of disciples so determined, that Christianity gained a toehold as a world religion. Then, after a converted Jew named Paul and the first pope, Peter, took the theology to Rome, it slowly rose to become the ruling faith of the empire. It has since fractured and fissured with various orthodoxies and Protestant denominations rejecting the rule of Roman Catholicism, but in the 21st millennium—as Christians measure it—Christianity remains the world's largest religion.

Jesus' people were from Nazareth, a modest, even overlooked village. Jesus performed his first miracle, changing water into wine, nearby. Today, Nazareth, still bucolic in places but with a total population of 60,000, is Israel's largest Arab city.

In the **Christian** Holy Land

In Bethlehem, Jerusalem and throughout the surrounding
hills and valleys, the path and passion of Jesus can be traced.

Was Jesus born
two millennia ago
in a stable or cave in
Bethlehem (left),
a town five miles
south of Jerusalem
in the Judean Hills?
Some doubt this,
thinking Nazareth
more likely for a
Nazarean and noting
that the sanctification
of Bethlehem seems
too convenient a way
to fulfill a prophecy
that the Messiah
would come from
Bethlehem. But a
majority opinion in
the Christian Bible's
New Testament,
and throughout the
Christian world,
is that Bethlehem
is where Jesus' life
and saga began.

The Sea of Galilee—
actually a 64-square-
mile freshwater lake
in a depression of
the Jordan River—
supported several
vibrant cities in Jesus'
day. Five of his 12
disciples were from
villages on the
Galilean shore, and
Mary Magdalene
came from a Galilean
town as well. Jesus
preached here often;
nearby, he delivered
the Sermon on the
Mount ("Blessed are
the meek . . . "). Here,
he turned five loaves
of bread and two fish
into a meal for many.
Jesus calmed Galilee's
waters. He even
walked upon them.

Denis Waugh

Erich Lessing/Art Resource

Richard T. Nowitz

From birth to death:
In Bethlehem's
Church of the Nativity,
an ornate star marks
the site traditionally
regarded as the spot
where Jesus was born.
In Jerusalem, a Greek
Orthodox priest lights
a candle and a woman
pays obeisance at
the door of the Church
of the Holy Sepulchre,
which honors the
place where Christ
was crucified.

Alfred Yaghobzadeh/Sipa

Richard T. Nowitz (3)

A ridge in Jerusalem called the Mount of Olives was visited by biblical figures, from the prophet Ezekiel to King David to Jesus. On one slope, in the serene Garden of Gethsemane (above), Jesus was betrayed by Judas. After Jesus' death and subsequent resurrection, he appeared to his disciples on the road to Emmaus, not far away (today, in el-Qubeibeh, left). From atop the mount, the church of St. Mary Magdalene is a grand image set against the ancient city (right).

Who Was **Muhammad**?

In a volatile age there emerged a serene, strong leader who bequeathed to his people a treatise so moving and wise that it became the bedrock of Islam. Muhammad said he was merely the agent. The Koran was the word of Allah.

اول الصوندوغك يرمشرقيدرمغربميدرثاميدر روميم

قيغى اقليم در أنى سكا بلدورم د دى مينه خاتون ايدراوغلمى

كوردم كيم اول لكنك ورتا مسنه الصوندى برجيران ولدوم

كه بوشيمدى طوغان اوغلان سوزنجه فهم ايلدى اولوكشى

In Islamic art, icons and living things are not to be depicted lest the artist challenge Allah's place or vision. These 16th century Turkish pictures show the infant Muhammad with angels, and (opposite) praying at the Kaaba.

H e was descended from Abraham through Ishmael in a line that included many prophets—but none after him, for he was destined to become the Seal of the Prophets. Muhammad was born nearly six centuries after another great philosopher, Jesus of Nazareth, spawned a cult that bloomed into a durable religion. As with Jesus, there was little—except perhaps his name, which means "highly praised"—in Muhammad's early years to indicate that this man would found a discipline for the ages. Mecca, a desert city in what is now Saudi Arabia, was a sea of strife in the late 6th century, and when Muhammad's parents died young, the boy was adopted by an uncle. Muslim tradition tells us that Muhammad's heart was infused at an early age with light, love, charity and all manner of pure-heartedness.

The Meccan environment, chaotic religiously as well as sociologically, and dominated by a variety of polytheisms, was not a setting likely to nurture such a character. As a young adult, this mattered little to Muhammad, a benign soul working in the caravan trade who married at age 25. It would be another 15 years before he began preaching in earnest. What happened in the interval is crucial: He went regularly to a cave outside Mecca to contemplate, to question the superstitions of his age and to pray. He wondered about Allah, a supreme god to many Meccans. Eventually, Muhammad became convinced that Allah was the only one— the God. "*La ilaha illa 'llah!*" was the tenet Muhammad brought down from the mount. There is no god but God.

Now came the Night of Power. In the cave, an angel came to Muhammad and charged him to "Proclaim! In the name of thy Lord and Cherisher,

Who Was **Muhammad**?

In these illustrations from *Progress of the Prophet,* Muhammad is visited by the archangel Gabriel; he and his followers are greeted by the Muslims of Yathrib; and, finally, he is visited by the Angel of Death, who escorts him to heaven.

Who created—Created man, out of a clot of congealed blood: Proclaim! And thy Lord Is Most Bountiful—He Who taught the Pen—Taught man that which he knew not [Koran 96:1–5]." So began Muhammad's rendering of the Book, the Koran, the holy narrative of Islam delivered by the angel . . . the word of Allah, by Allah.

Allah would dictate words to Muhammad during the remaining 22 years of the Prophet's life. His lessons, which implored listeners to forsake evil—licentiousness, greed, avarice—certainly did not fall as revelation upon the greater populace; in three years, Muhammad had only a few dozen converts. He, like Jesus before him, was preaching outside the box, and like Jesus in Jerusalem, he got into trouble in Mecca.

He fled, and the year of his flight—622 by

Christian reckoning—is regarded as year zero by Muslims. He went to Yathrib, subsequently called Medinat al-Nabi, "the city of the Prophet" and then, simply, Medina, the city. There, he lived in a humble clay house while continually, through his teachings, commandeering the minds of his new townsfolk. Finally, the great majority of citizenry came to revere its new leader and backed him wholeheartedly when he challenged Mecca for the soul of Arabia. He won, he lost, and then, eight years after he had left Mecca, he returned in ultimate triumph. He immediately forgave the Meccans, and in short order went to the Kaaba, a temple that was said to have been built by Abraham himself. Muhammad rededicated the Kaaba as the holy heart of Islam.

In 632 A.D., he died in Medina. In the next century, Muslim armies washed over Armenia, Iraq, most of North Africa including Egypt and Lebanon, Palestine, Persia, Spain and Syria. Muhammad had given the Arabs a religion, and today it is the second largest in the world.

Completed circa 692, the Dome of the Rock, a rotunda on an octagonal base in Jerusalem, is the oldest extant Muslim shrine. It is from here that Muhammad ascended to heaven at the end of his Night Journey. Nearby are the al-Aqsa Mosque, the Western Wall and the Church of the Holy Sepulchre.

In the **Muslim** Holy Land

Muhammad's life was lived in two places principally—Mecca and Medina. But as Abraham's descendant, Muhammad is of Canaan, too.

Within the Great Mosque in Mecca is Islam's most sacred shrine, the Kaaba, which all of Islam faces five times a day for prayer. Every Muslim must come here once, circumambulate the Kaaba seven times, then touch and kiss the Black Stone, set in a corner of the Kaaba. In 630, Muhammad removed pagan symbols from the Kaaba, covered here by a black curtain.

Kazuyoshi Nomachi/PPS

In the late 16th century, the Ottoman Sultan Murad III commissioned an illustrated manuscript based on Mustafa Darir's *Siyar-i Nabi*, or *Life of the Prophet*, written two centuries earlier. The massive project resulted in one of the greatest works of Islamic art. Because the story was not considered scripture, the illustrations didn't violate Muslim law (though even with the Prophet's face veiled, some conservatives may be offended). The illustrations on pages 52 through 55 are from the Sultan's commission, as is the one above. In this scene, set in Medina, adherents are at work on a building that will serve as both Muhammad's home and a mosque. The Prophet helps with construction, which utilizes mudbrick and the trunks and leaves of palms. The site was chosen when Muhammad let loose his camel and waited to see where the beast came to rest. Across the years, the mosque has often been enlarged. Today it is a hundred times the size of the original, and 260,000 worshipers may be housed, as in the Friday congregational prayer at right.

The Mosque of the
Prophet is second
only to Mecca as a
sacred place for
Muslims, who visit in
great numbers each
year. Above, the
devout depart after
the *maghrib,* or
evening, prayers.
A huge extension of
the mosque, finished
in 1995, provides air
conditioning
(opposite) for the
hot summer days.
Including those who
pray outside in an
area covered in
marble, worshipers
can number a million.

On Mount Hira (opposite), outside Mecca, Muhammad received his first revelation from the archangel Gabriel. The Prophet used the cave beneath the white stone for meditation. Above: Muslims believe Adam and Eve met in the Plains of Arafat, in the present day Saudi Arabia. Water cools pilgrims (and trees) in the heat. The Kaaba's Black Stone, right, is the symbol of Allah's covenant with Adam.

Pilgrims
Through the Ages

Politics and war may have redrawn boundaries in the Middle East, but holy land has always been homeland, calling to the devout. These pilgrims answered, braving any foe and traveling any distance to pay homage.

For centuries, Jews were on foreign soil in Jerusalem, guests of Muslims, Ottomans or whoever else ruled Palestine. Efforts to reestablish a Jewish nation started up in the late 1800s, about when the photo at left was taken. Above, in 1908, also at the Western Wall.

Christians, visitors in the land of Christ's birth, return to biblical settings to honor their lord and savior. Left: In 1899 a christening in the Jordan River recalls the baptism of Jesus by John the Baptist. Below: a year later, on the road to Jericho. Right: Also in 1900, priests reenact scenes from Christ's passion by carrying a great cross through the Via Dolorosa in Jerusalem.

In 1908, Muslims parade through Jerusalem (left). At the time, the city and indeed all of Palestine was in the hands of the Ottoman Turks, the great majority of whom were followers of Islam. Right: The Dome of the Rock attracted a steady stream of pilgrims a century ago, as it does today. Below: Then as now, Mecca was, of course, the ultimate destination for Muslims. A caravan of Persian pilgrims, bound for the sacred city, establish a camp at the ancient port of Jaffa, which is now part of Israel's largest urban center, Tel Aviv.

Holy **War**

Whose land is this? In the 20th century, that difficult question was posed, over and over, against the echo of gunfire.

With the city of Jerusalem as a backdrop in January 1948, three armed Arabs scan the Silwan Valley for any Jewish opposition.

ancor between religions is hardly uncommon, and the history of Jews and Muslims is no exception. Whether the discord stems from religious differences, economic rivalry or, ironically, from a chafing similarity—brother against brother—in today's struggle, a plot of land provides a point of detonation. Because the geography involved is relatively small, it is all too easy for the principals to bump into each other, and in this part of the world, push is invariably followed by shove.

There have been, in years past, many instances of Jews living harmoniously within larger Islamic states. Indeed, these places have generally been considered preferable to enclaves within Christian lands. But seeking shelter as a subordinate culture within a Muslim territory and operating as a separate, powerful state are quite different.

This nation-state, now called Israel, took root in the late 1800s when disenfranchised Russian Jews

At right, in February 1948, terror grips Jerusalem's Ben Yehuda Street after an Arab bomb kills 57 and wounds more than 100. That same year, a ship bearing orphans from Eastern Europe pulls into Haifa. From 1917, when the British wrested Palestine from the Ottomans, to 1948, the number of Jews living in that region increased tenfold.

settled in Palestine, leading to a Zionist tenet that the land was rightfully theirs. The inherent problems could not have surprised them; early on, Asher Ginzberg, an influential Zionist, wrote (under the pen name Ahad Haam) that Palestine was too small and bore the challenge of a large native population. Nevertheless, the seemingly perpetual clock

of contention had been set in motion.

After World War I, the League of Nations gave Great Britain a mandate over Palestine, which had long been under Ottoman rule. In the preamble to the mandate was the 1917 Balfour Declaration, whereby Britain supported the Jewish effort to secure a homeland in Palestine. But the mandate proved only to be an incubator for tension and flare-ups. After WWII, Britain decided to pass the problem along to the U.N., which in 1947 called for dividing the region into two separate states. Zionists were pleased, at least momentarily, but Palestinians and Arabs were appalled by the emergence of a Western-like domain in their midst. They

The relatively new United Nations shouldered the onerous task of monitoring the 1949 truce. The U.N. also provided many refugees with aid and housing, as here in December 1953 at a school for Palestinian refugees near Jericho.

responded with guns: Just one day after Israel declared itself a nation in May 1948, Arab forces from Egypt, Syria, Jordan, Lebanon and Iraq attacked. Intense fighting alternated with truces until, in early '49, an armistice was reached with all but Iraq. For the Israelis, the fighting resulted in the destruction of important agricultural areas. For the Arabs, it was a far worse nightmare. They had been humiliated by the army of a new country, which ended up gaining land, including West Jerusalem. Even worse, in what is still referred to as "the disaster," hundreds of thousands of Palestinians fled their homes and ended up in an area controlled by Jordan—the West Bank. The refugee debacle has ever since been a tinderbox in the Middle East.

During the next few years there were intermittent clashes, but the truce somehow held until 1956, when Egypt nationalized the Suez Canal. Israel felt menaced by the Soviet-backed buildup of Egyptian forces, led by President Gamal Abdel Nasser. In October, Israel's Moshe Dayan led a sortie into the Sinai Peninsula. Britain and France, in concert with the Israelis, joined in two days later. Finally the U.N.—at the behest of the Americans and Soviets—halted the fighting, but not before Israel had taken the Gaza Strip. Bowing to international pressure, Israel relinquished Sinai and Gaza in '57 while retaining vital access to the Gulf of Aqaba. For his part, Nasser cleverly parlayed defeat into victory by consolidating the Muslim world in his battle against Zionism.

Fighting was relatively light for several years; then, in 1964, after Israel had nearly completed a project to divert water from the Jordan River to the Negev Desert, Syria started work on a similar operation near the river's headwaters. This facility would seriously diminish the Israeli water supply, so Israel promptly destroyed the facility, and tempers on both sides grew shorter and shorter.

In 1967, after a string of skirmishes and provocations—for example, the Soviets told Syria that the Israelis were massing troops near its border, which probably wasn't so—matters again came to

Gilles Caron/Gamma

a head. Israel, infuriated that Egypt had sealed off the Gulf of Aqaba and feeling threatened by its troops in the Sinai, launched a preemptive air strike against the Soviet-built Egyptian air force, much of which never left the ground. Within three hours, most of Egypt's planes and air bases were demolished. It was June 5, the beginning of what is known by Israelis as the Six-Day War, and called by Arabs the Setback. By the time the U.N. secured a cease-fire, the Israeli victory, a masterpiece of thrusts and counterthrusts, had stunned the world.

The Star of David now flew over Gaza, Sinai, the strategically located Golan Heights and the West Bank of the Jordan River, including East Jerusalem. The latter was of the utmost importance. For Israel, East Jerusalem—the Old City, with its holy sites— is at the crux of Judaism and is simply not a point for negotiation. For the Palestinians, their historic territorial claims and the holy sites there make it a

These photos were taken in 1967 during the crucial Six-Day War. At top left, Israeli infantrymen on the Via Dolorosa in Jerusalem's Old City advance block by block. Bottom, a soldier kisses the Western Wall. The photograph at right was taken near the Nile by a low-flying Israeli pilot. As the shadow of his Mirage jet approaches, four Egyptians take what cover they can.

David Rubinger (2)

A wounded Israeli soldier (opposite) receives treatment and a kind word from a bloodied buddy at an aid station during the Yom Kippur War in 1973. Above, Israeli soldiers fire a 175mm cannon in the Golan Heights. This war severely damaged the Israeli economy and led to the resignation of Prime Minister Golda Meir.

point on which they simply will not compromise.

Saddled with another frustrating defeat, the Arab world began to embrace the three-year-old Palestine Liberation Organization. With their armies wrecked, Arab states began siphoning funds to the PLO. Thus were financed forays into Israel and its occupied lands. Israel responded with actions against the organization's host countries, Jordan and Lebanon. Nevertheless, the PLO had used the Six-Day War as a springboard to the realm of international powerbrokering.

In 1970, Nasser was succeeded by Anwar Sadat, who grew increasingly disturbed by diplomatic failures to alter Israel's dominance in the region. Sadat entered into negotiations with Syrian President Hafiz Assad. On October 6, 1973, with the support of six other Arab nations, Egypt and Syria launched surprise attacks. It was Yom Kippur, the most sacred of Jewish holy days, as well as the 10th day of Ramadan, the anniversary of a famed battle fought by the prophet Muhammad. The Israelis, caught off-guard, had to petition the U.S. for help. With its

massive dependence on oil, America didn't want to exacerbate relations with Arab oil-producing states, but when it was learned that the Soviets were supplying matériel to Egypt and Syria, President Richard Nixon ordered an airlift of weapons to Israel "to maintain a balance of forces and achieve stability in the Middle East."

In the end, the result was, once again, the same. After initial losses, Israel emerged victorious and annexed more land, which it later ceded as a result of U.S. pressure. But the Yom Kippur War opened the way for diplomatic talks that came to fruition in 1979 with the Camp David Accords, whereby Israel returned the Sinai Peninsula to Egypt, which in turn recognized the right of Israel to exist.

It was a grand achievement, but the habitual hostilities were not so easily vanquished. In 1982, Israel, trying to wipe out the PLO, invaded Lebanon, which had been harboring the terrorist group. PLO guerrillas were routed but merely found other sites from which to unleash their hostilities.

The late '80s gave rise to a development that,

Catherine Leroy

Israel went all out in its effort to destroy the PLO in Lebanon in 1982. Above: Beirut under fire. The Israelis managed to drive Yasir Arafat to Tunisia but ended up in a three-year quagmire. Below: the funeral of a teenage Jewish girl at a West Bank settlement in 1987. Opposite, in '88, the _intifadeh_.

Allan Tannenbaum

with hindsight, seems inevitable. The Palestinian people themselves, boiling over after two decades of Israeli occupation—and abetted by Hamas and others—launched an _intifadeh,_ an uprising that involved violence, demonstrations, strikes and boycotts of Israeli goods. The televised images of Palestinians hurling stones at the heavily armed Israeli soldiers provided an interesting counterpoint to the David and Goliath tale in the Old Testament—as the Palestinians were no doubt aware.

Other accords would follow, notably the Oslo and Wye pacts, but the bloodletting continues. In a land where religion and politics have taken the form of impregnable alloys, where fervent people strive desperately after sovereignty and self-determination, the symbols, the methods and the land itself have intertwined in an endless tapestry of zealous self-righteousness. If the images coming from Israel and the West Bank during the past several months seem freshly horrifying, the news is nothing new.

Alfred Yaghobzadeh/Sipa

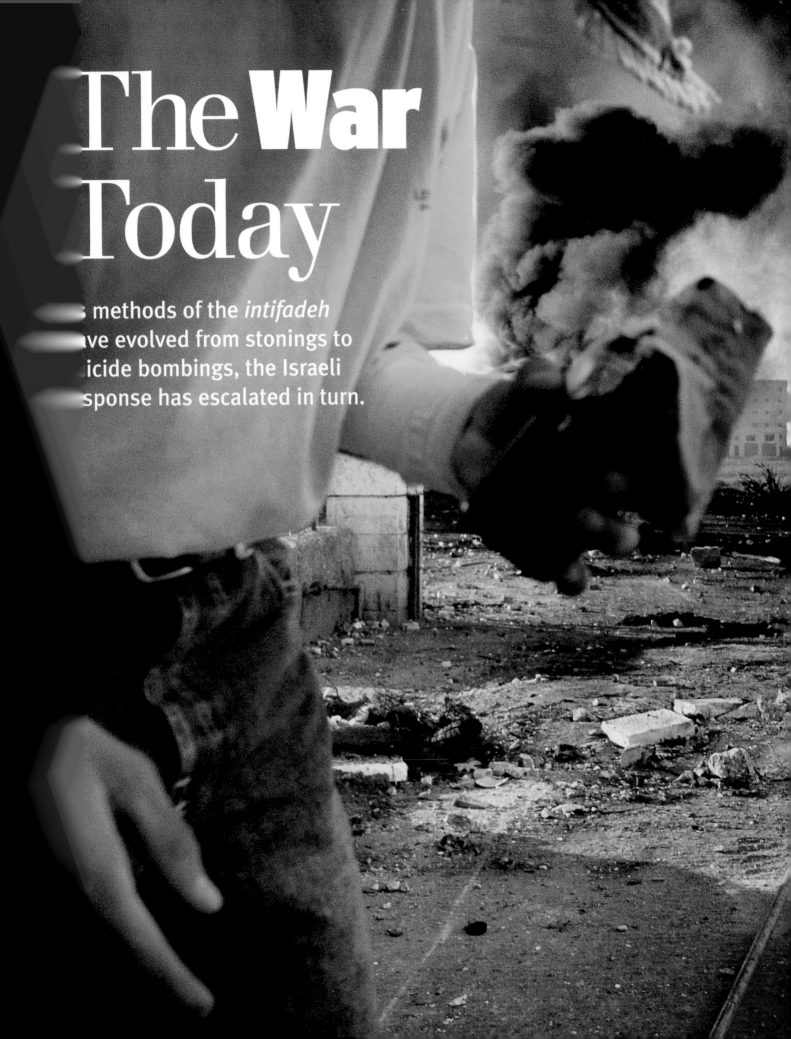

The War Today

methods of the *intifadeh*
ve evolved from stonings to
icide bombings, the Israeli
sponse has escalated in turn.

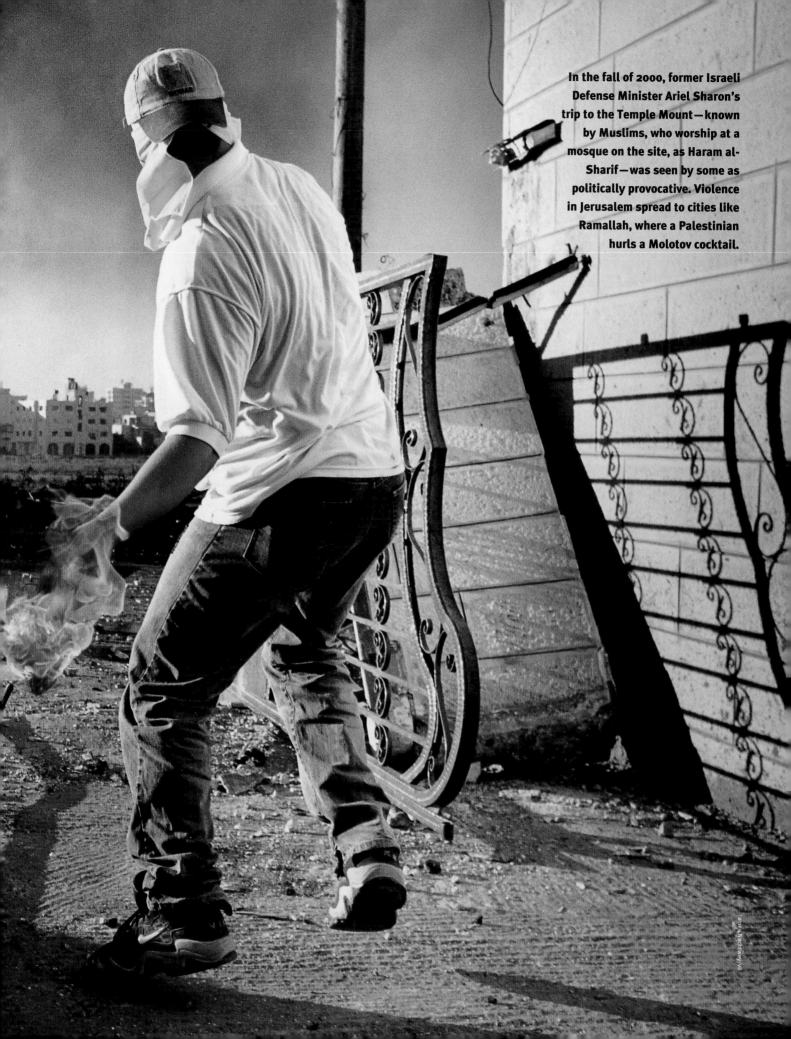

In the fall of 2000, former Israeli Defense Minister Ariel Sharon's trip to the Temple Mount—known by Muslims, who worship at a mosque on the site, as Haram al-Sharif—was seen by some as politically provocative. Violence in Jerusalem spread to cities like Ramallah, where a Palestinian hurls a Molotov cocktail.

In June 2002, a Palestinian woman in Gaza City, on the Gaza Strip, cautiously peers around the side of a house at an Israeli tank. Nearby lies the Jewish Netzarim settlement, one of about 150 in the West Bank, Golan Heights and Gaza that have sprung up since 1967. They are a wellspring of unrest.

In the not-distant past, there was a ray of hope. Under 1993's Oslo Accords, Israel and the PLO agreed to work for "interdependence," in which Palestine, with self-rule in the Gaza Strip and the West Bank, would be seen as a "partner" in the region, not an "inferior." Then, as ever, things fell apart.

In 1996, bombings by Islamic militants killed dozens, and when Israel opened a tourist tunnel near the al-Aqsa Mosque in Jerusalem, some Palestinians, sensing an attempt to extend sovereignty over a disputed area, took to the streets. More than 50 Palestinians and a dozen Israelis were slain. Another relative lull was followed in 2000 by the area's worst violence in 30 years when, in the week after Sharon's visit to the Temple Mount/Haram al-Sharif, 70 were killed and 1,800 injured.

In 2001 and '02, the main Palestinian method of attack in the *intifadeh* became suicide bombing, and the world looked on horrified as men, women and children were killed in terrible explosions on buses, in cafes and at schools. Some Islamic imams, hoping to stop the carnage, pointed to the Koran and said the bombings violated the teachings of Muhammad, who condemned suicide. The argument in defense of the tactic viewed the bombings as an act of martyrdom. With cultures and theological interpretations clashing, the war raged on.

An Israeli Defense Force soldier at the Kalandia checkpoint in Palestine surveys the traffic passing from the West Bank town of Ramallah into Jerusalem. For the Israelis, checkpoints are a necessary cog in the never-ending effort to impede the movements of dangerous individuals. To the Palestinians, they are yet one more indignity.

The scene at right has become all too common.
On March 21, 2002, an explosion went off in a
busy Jerusalem shopping district. A Palestinian
suicide bomber was the instrument of death.
The woman above is Dareen Abu Aeshah. Her
family made this photograph available on
February 28, 2002, one day after the 22-year-old
Palestinian blew herself up at a West Bank
checkpoint, wounding three Israeli policemen in
the process. A month earlier, 28-year-old Wafa
Idris became the first female suicide bomber
when she killed an 81-year-old Israeli man and
injured more than 150 others in West Jerusalem.
It was certain she would not be the last. As a
friend of Idris told Reuters, "the level of Israeli
suppression and degradation against us are
creating thousands of Wafas." Saddam Hussein
called for a memorial to be built in her honor in
a main square of Baghdad.

In August 2002, a member of the Israeli funeral service searches the area around a shattered bus in northern Israel's Mount Meiron. A suicide bomber turned the bus into a fireball, killing at least nine people. Suicide attacks have occurred for centuries, but the first in the Israeli-Palestinian conflict took place on April 16, 1993. Since then, more than a hundred bombers have taken their own lives and those of hundreds of others. Most of the bombs are made out of triacetone-triperoxide (also found in shoe-bomber suspect Richard Reid's sneakers). *Time* called the explosive "simple to produce."

Another bus, another bomb. This time in June 2002, this time in Jerusalem, this time with 19 dead, like this woman with the police ID tag. Why would someone kill total strangers and remove himself from the ranks of the living? For a long time, Palestinians harbored the hope that they would one day exercise self-rule. But years of living in a state of occupation have produced a frustrated, angry people with no one left to lean on. The PLO has failed in its goals. The "enemy," Israel, has the upper hand and the weapons to maintain it. It used to be that suicide bombers were young men, religious zealots with no hopes beyond the virgins in heaven that await the martyr. Today, the bombers are often more mainstream, with something to live for, and four fifths of the people in the Gaza Strip approve of their efforts— however extreme—to attain dignity and to exact vengeance.

Yannis Behrakis/Reuters/Landov

With its citizenry continually subjected to suicide bombings and other forms of terrorism, the government of Israel has responded in a variety of ways, including house-to-house searches. Here, in a refugee camp in the West Bank town of Tulkarem, a Palestinian woman stands by as an Israeli soldier climbs through her bedroom window in search of militants or weapons. Later, loudspeakers demand that all males between the ages of 15 and 45 report for interrogation.

David Silverman/Getty

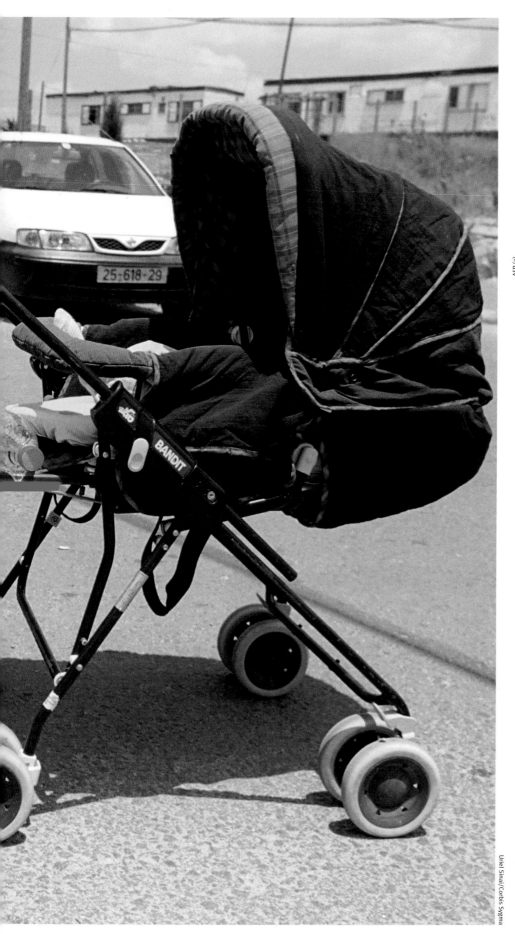

Two Israeli women and a child warily cross the street in a West Bank settlement in June 2002, days after five people were shot dead there. A civilian toting an automatic weapon is a familiar sight in settlements. The Palestinians consider these communities occupied land; many Israelis regard them as "retrieved." Below, a TV camera captures a Palestinian and his boy caught in a cross fire near the Netzarim Jewish settlement in 2000. The boy was killed.

The second *intifadeh* has been significantly more violent as Palestinians have increasingly turned to suicide bombings. In June 2001, however, it was a rock cast by a Palestinian that struck the fatal blow against five-month-old Yehuda Shoham, who had been riding in his father's car. (Left, the child's funeral.) Many people have questioned how such devoutly religious people can justify suicide bombing. What about the Koran? While it usually teaches benevolence, the book also sometimes encourages a fight. In the 22nd chapter of the Koran, it states, "To those against whom war is made, permission is given to fight," referring specifically to "those who have been expelled from their homes . . . for no cause except that they say, 'Our Lord is Allah.'"

It is a conflict that drags on and on and on, a source of grief for an untold many. Here, in April 2001, relatives provide what solace they can to the sister of Wael Khweitar, a 27-year-old Palestinian soldier who was also a physician. He was killed in an Israeli raid on the Gaza Strip. Menace, even death, daily prowls the byways of these troubled holy lands.

Damir Sagolj/Reuters/Landov

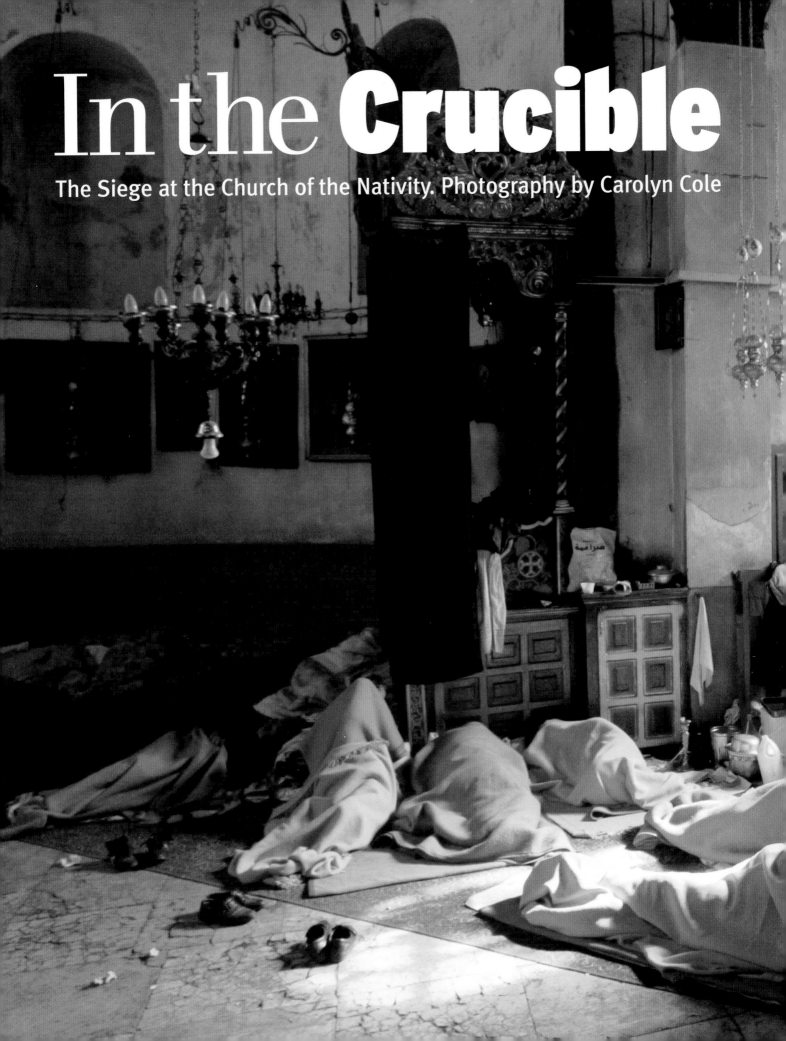

In the **Crucible**

The Siege at the Church of the Nativity. Photography by Carolyn Cole

On April 2, 2002, as the drama was beginning to unfold, what did each of them see? The Palestinian militants who no longer considered themselves safe in Bethlehem's Manger Square or across the way in the Omar Mosque finally realized there was an ultimate sanctuary: the Church of the Nativity, a place so venerated that the Israelis would never dare invade it. The Christian priests, nuns and monks inside the compound saw a sacred site imperiled, and took it upon themselves to do whatever was possible to save it. The Israeli soldiers, peering out of tanks or through rifle sights, saw a church that looked more like an antiquated fortress, an old stone facade they could easily take down but that was, at the same time, inviolable.

If the most recent troubles required a symbolic nexus to bring affairs into sharp focus, they got one in the spring when Israeli efforts against Palestinians in Arab-controlled Bethlehem led to a 39-day siege—Christian clerics and Palestinians on the inside, Israeli artillery and sharpshooters on the outside. The situation was as weighted with meaning as it was fraught with tension. The Israeli high command debated daily how to proceed, while countries well beyond the usual ones—not just the United States but Spain, Austria, Greece, Luxembourg and Ireland—volunteered or were recruited in an effort to end the standoff. In Rome, Pope John Paul II, who theretofore had been imploring religions outside his own to find some way to peace in the Middle East, now found himself praying for priests and nuns.

It was a complicated, terrible, yet strangely elegant situation, staged in the most inevitable of settings. When 30 gunmen burst through the doors of the compound's Franciscan monastery on April 2 and were followed in by more than 200 Palestinian

A month into the siege, *Los Angeles Times* photographer Carolyn Cole rushed into the church with 10 aid workers. She stayed until the end, recording the ever more desperate situation. Previous pages: Palestinians rest in the basilica. Above and opposite: A slit in the Door of Humility allows a glimpse of a tank.

Opposite: As dawn breaks above the altar, a Palestinian takes his tea while a compatriot sleeps huddled in blankets. Above: With food all but gone, Palestinian policeman Najee Abu Abed eats lemon leaves gathered in a rear courtyard.

police and civilians, it was impossible for them to know what a resonant chapter they were writing in the remarkable history of this church—this place.

Bethlehem is today a city of 100,000, a mere five miles from Jerusalem. It has always been about religion. The small cave within the Church of the Nativity's grotto, where it is said Jesus was born, was, according to archaeological evidence, a sacred site long before the Christian era. At the cave, the Greek god Adonis was celebrated. In Genesis, Bethlehem (or Ephratah) was where Rachel, Jacob's second wife, was buried. David was a shepherd

there when Samuel was sent by God to Bethlehem to anoint the boy as successor to King Saul.

Two of the Synoptic Gospel writers, Matthew and Luke (though not the earliest, Mark), say that Jesus was born in Bethlehem. Some scholars see Nazareth, where he grew up, as a likelier birthplace, but ever since St. Justin Martyr cited the spot in the grotto in the 2nd century A.D., the cave and its town have occupied a place of primacy in Christianity's geographical history. A church was built atop the cave in 326 A.D., then destroyed two centuries later in an uprising. It was replaced by a larger basil-

Father Parthenios (left) and Father Vissarion bless the church on the Greek Orthodox Easter. On the mattress are Jihad Jaara (right), nursing a bullet wound in his ankle, and Abdallah Dawood. Both men were exiled after the siege ended.

ica that would weather many storms through nearly 15 centuries. It was attacked, seized and regained by Muslim and Christian armies both before and during the Crusades. The violence visited upon the region in that time—Christian crusaders "rode in blood up to their knees" while slaughtering 40,000 Muslims and Jews in Jerusalem in 1099—indicates not only a long tradition of holy war in the Middle East but also the Church of the Nativity's miraculous ability to stand its ground. It was the one major church in the country to survive a Persian invasion in 614; it survived the Crusades; it survives today as one of the oldest Christian churches in the world.

On April 1, 2002, a relatively placid world lay behind the church's entrance, the tiny Door of Humility. That world existed within the boundaries of a 14,000-square-yard complex and included the basilica, an assemblage of Christian institutions (a Greek Orthodox convent, an Armenian convent, a Latin convent), and the grotto. And then, suddenly, there were gunmen coming through the doors. A shocking moment evolved, quite quickly, into a standoff, followed by a siege. While some few priests left in the first days of the episode, the great majority, along with dozens of nuns and monks, determined to stay, strategizing that this would give the church a better chance against desecration or destruction. Israeli snipers took occasional, and occasionally successful, shots when Palestinians ventured into the courtyard. Inside, Palestinians cooked food within the basilica's altar and washed dishes in the baptismal font. But when the priests asked that no one sleep in the nativity grotto, their guests complied. The Christian clerics kept to their own quarters by night, while Palestinians slept on the church's stone floor. At one point some crucifixes were stolen. When the issue was raised, they were returned. Eventually, the food ran out.

The world watched, rapt and fearful, while commentators from all camps spoke of the ironies and intersections of what was happening. "The Church was ostensibly built to honor a Jew and his family," pointed out the Freeman Center's pro-Israel Middle

At first, Christian clerics were opposed to Muslims praying toward Mecca in the main sanctuary of the basilica, but they relented. Still, said Father Parthenios, "I didn't get used to it." The prayer sessions, at 4:30 a.m., 12 noon and 7:30 p.m. each day, created an extraordinary disconnect or, depending upon one's point of view, a vision of ecumenical brotherhood. The man in the back, Allah Barakat, crouches rather than kneels owing to back and nerve problems incurred in an accident when he was a member of Yasir Arafat's security force.

East commentator, Emanuel A. Winston. It was noted that Muslims had been granted access to the church for 14 centuries; there was no need to be brandishing guns. Latin patriarch of Jerusalem Michel Sabbah, the head of the Roman Catholic church in the region, issued a subtle warning to the Israeli army, calling the basilica a "place of refuge for everyone."

So it remained for 39 days. Negotiations far from Bethlehem finally led to a brokered settlement: 13 Palestinian militants would be flown to Cyprus on British military planes, thence to exile in a variety of European nations. The 124 other Palestinians who had not already left the church would be free to go. The tanks would pull back.

Hard-liners on both sides condemned the pact, Israelis insisting the "senior terrorists" should have been taken in Bethlehem, Palestinians saying it

Palestinians wait as negotiations continue. The accord's terms include handing over weapons to the U.S. An AK-47's serial number is recorded in hopes of recovering the gun one day.

Above: Emotions run high as the names of those to be exiled are read aloud. Ibrahim Abeiyat (opposite), the Israelis' Most Wanted man, was sent to Spain. Just before the standoff ended, Khalaf Najazeh (right) was shot by an automated Israeli sniper crane: the last to die in the siege.

would have been nobler for their own to die in the church. But most others everywhere were relieved. Pietro Sambi, the Vatican's Jerusalem representative, entered the church shortly after the Palestinians had left, surveyed the mess and the scant damage, and declared that no formal desecration had taken place. A Muslim whose son was even then being flown to Cyprus visited the church that ultimate day. Saheeya Khamees said a prayer of thanks to the Virgin Mary for protecting her militant son during the siege. And she thanked Mary a second time for preserving the church.

Christianity's Dwindling Influence

The Christian population in
the region is evaporating,
as is any Christian authority.
A papal pilgrimage to the
Holy Land proved the point.

He, the most traveled pope in the history of the world, made his 91st international trip with three things in mind: personal spiritual enrichment, reconciliation among the three faiths descended from Abraham, and peace in the Holy Land. In early spring of the Christian Jubilee year 2000, Pope John Paul II went to trace the footsteps of Jesus, and to reiterate Christ's thoughts on the value of forgiveness, the magic of brotherhood and the need for turning the other cheek—while never presuming that he might play an active role in negotiations. "The Holy See does not want to interfere," said Father Remi Hoeckman, the pope's point man on Catholic-Jewish relations, while adding, "We want to reach a point at which the Holy Land can set an example for the rest of humankind, which it's definitely not doing right now. If . . . in spite of a painful past we can speak with one voice, it is a sign for humankind to rediscover bonds among human beings."

The pontiff, at 79, was still considered a strong moral voice in much of the world, and he was treated respectfully by most of his hosts. It is true that Saddam Hussein would not allow John Paul into Iraq to visit the site of ancient Ur, where Abraham is said to have been born, and that some Israeli and Palestinian leaders used audiences with the pope to promote grievances or assert absolute claim to Jerusalem. But, generally, the journey went well. In a celebrated gesture, the pope took the text of an apology for Christian misdeeds that he had delivered earlier at St. Peter's and left it at the Western

In Jordan, the pope gazes over the Holy Land from the spot on Mount Nebo where, according to scripture, God allowed Moses to view, but not to enter. John Paul, by contrast, was allowed to pray and preach in Israel—but to what effect?

the Church of the Holy Sepulchre in Jerusalem, where Catholics and the Eastern churches believe Jesus was buried and resurrected. (Protestants hold with the nearby Garden Tomb.)

Even when trouble threatened, it bowed to the presence of the pope. Nazareth's Church of the Annunciation is said to be the place where Gabriel told Mary that she would give birth to the Messiah. In 1999, when the city's Christian minority objected to a mosque being built nearby, riots broke out. In 2000, there were concerns that violence would attend the pope's Mass on March 25. But a local Muslim prayer-leader's call for calm prevailed.

The pope was, of course, just passing through, and as he did, there were trailing signs that the deference shown him was just that—deference—and nothing more substantial. John Paul went with Yasir Arafat to Deheisha, a ghetto of a camp outside Jerusalem. Some of the 10,000 residents had been refugees from the 1948 war and still had keys to houses they had once fled. The big issue in Deheisha was reparation, but all the pope could offer was, "I hope and pray that my visit will bring some comfort in your difficult situation." The young men of Deheisha were unmoved, and that night rioted in the streets. Later in the year, with the pope long since back in Rome, the second *intifadeh* began.

If confirmation were needed that Christianity's influence in the land of Christ's birth had all but evaporated, the results of John Paul's pilgrimage provided it. But this should have surprised no one. The pope was, after all, preaching in a land of many Christian relics and sites but, today, precious few Christians. A 1,300-year rise of Islam had already eroded the Christian population among Arabs before the 20th century, and then as troubles between Muslims and Jews intensified, the erosion accelerated. In 1946, 13 percent of Palestine was Christian; by 2000, the figure for the region was a minuscule 2.1 percent, half Orthodox, half Roman Catholic. As Christians have absented themselves, there have been consequences, an obvious one being that warring parties are left to sort things out by themselves with no mediating voice. In his book *The Body and the Blood,* Charles Sennott writes, "If the Christians disappear, the Middle East will become that much more vulnerable to this embittered dichotomy." John Paul's experience raises the question: How much more vulnerable can it get?

Above: On March 25, the pontiff prays at Nazareth's Grotto of the Annunciation. Opposite: He inserts in the Western Wall words to the Jews that he had read in Rome. Wall. He visited Jordan, and was moved by the view of the Promised Land from Mount Nebo. Near the banks of the Jordan River he said to his companions, "In my mind I see Jesus coming to the waters not far from here to be baptized by John the Baptist. I see Jesus passing on his way to the Holy City, where he would die and rise again. I see him opening the eyes of the blind man as he passes by." The pope relived this life of Christ, going to Bethlehem, saying Mass to 80,000 from the site of the Sermon on the Mount, climbing the steps to the room where it is said the Last Supper was held, praying in the Garden of Gethsemane, celebrating a final Mass at

Two different Bibles and the Koran are the blocks upon which these religions rest. History is continually written and rewritten—violence ebbs and then it flows—but finally the faithful must return to the page, to the word of the Lord.

The Hebrew Bible

Written by divinely inspired authors between two and three millennia ago, this is the sacred scripture of Judaism. It is made up of three parts. The first is Torah—or Pentateuch, or "Law"—which sets forth religious and social rules, tells the story of the creation and describes the Lord's covenant with Israel, the Exodus from Egypt, and the Hebrew people's arrival in the Promised Land. Nevi'im ("Prophets") is the Israeli history in Palestine, filled not only with prophecies but with wars and heroes—principal among the latter, David. Ketuvim ("Writings") includes meditations on evil and death, as well as psalms and praises of Israel's covenant with God. The word "Bible" is derived from the Greek *Biblia* (the Book) and has no precise translation in Hebrew; Jews call their sacred volume Tanakh, an acronym for Torah, Nevi'im and Ketuvim. The Torah seen here was found on an archaeological expedition and now resides at Drew University in New Jersey.

The **Books** Endure

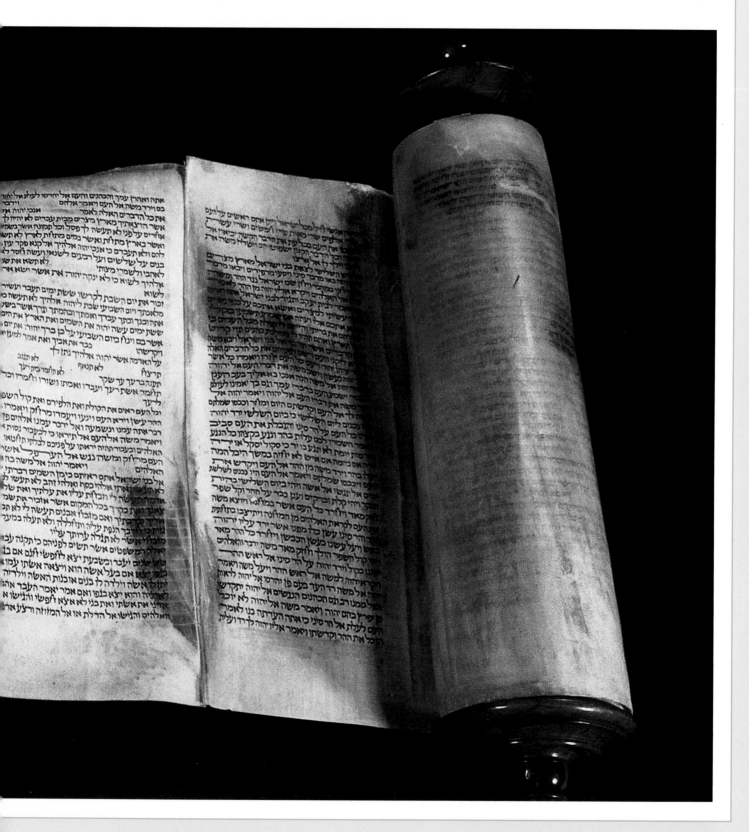

The Christian Bible

It is often said that the Old Testament of the Christian Bible equates with the entirety of the Hebrew Bible, but this is not the case. When the early Christians were assembling their book in the first century after Christ's crucifixion, they accepted the Jewish view of history as truth—with reservations. Working from a Greek translation of the Jewish Bible rather than from the Hebrew text, they incorporated nuanced changes that would prove crucial (for instance, the mother of the Messiah would be "a young woman," said the Hebrew word *almah,* but "a virgin," stipulated the Greek *parthenos*). The Christian Bible, seen here as printed by Gutenberg in 1455, reordered chapters and ignored or diminished some episodes sacred to Jews. And it added a New Testament, whose 27 books constituted a far shorter narrative than that of the Old, but which changed the entire message: Christ was the Messiah, so all that came before was leading to *him,* not to a still-prophesied savior.

Harry Benson

The Koran

Muhammad could neither read nor write, so he listened to Allah's words, then passed them along to his people orally. The stories and laws were not recorded in book form until after his death. In the Koran, which means "the Recitation," much of Jewish tradition is confirmed by Allah, as is the greatness of Jesus as a prophet (he foresees his successor, Muhammad). But Jesus as the son of God: This is blasphemy. And the Christian doctrine of a Holy Trinity—Father, Son and Holy Spirit—is seen as polytheistic (a very serious point, since Muhammad was converting an Arab world that was, before his rise, largely polytheistic). As with the Tanakh and the Bible, the Koran, a centuries-old version of which is seen here, stresses obedience to God (Allah) and sorrow for one's sins. It warns of Allah's final judgment and speaks of heaven and hell. As with the Old Testament, there is violence, sometimes meted out in Allah's name, but the Koran more often urges mercy and compassion.

And **Tomorrow**?

On a peaceful day at summer camp in Jerusalem, Shani Batut (left), an eight-year-old Israeli, plays with Rada Derhy, a 10-year-old Palestinian.

It is impossible to predict what the future holds for Israel, the West Bank and all of the Middle East. Some people dare to hope, and dare to act on that hope. During the summer of 2002, an Israeli-Palestinian organization called the Wellspring for Democratic Education ran a camp in Jerusalem for 160 children: 80 Palestinians and 80 Israelis. Held on the campus of Hebrew University, workshops and playtime for the kids were structured so that they would intermingle; then, in separate groups, they were taught about hatred and getting along, about war and peace. On July 17, the girls above idled away a sunny day, blissfully defiant of the animosity that had infected many of their kinfolk. If this image is sufficient to spur optimism, it needs to be noted: two weeks later, a bomb, detonated in the campus cafeteria, killed seven, five of whom were Jewish Americans. None of the children attending camp were physically harmed. But whatever lessons they were being taught, and whatever message their friendship sent, were buffeted, along with the summer calm.